WILD ANIMALS
of the CANADIAN ROCKIES

~ *by* ~

Kevin Van Tighem

Photography by Dennis & Esther Schmidt

Rocky
Mountain Books

VANCOUVER · VICTORIA · CALGARY

The Blackfoot say that Napi came here after he created the animals and taught people how to live. He came at last to a place where limestone walls rear high into the sky and newborn waters cascade from glaciers. In that place, there are grizzly tracks in the river mud. Wolves howl. Wild animals exhale the breath of their creator. It is like that there, even now.

Rocky Mountain Books
#108 – 17665 66A Avenue
Surrey, BC V3S 2A7
www.rmbooks.com

Rocky Mountain Books
PO Box 468
Custer, WA
98240-0468

Library and Archives Canada Cataloguing in Publication

Van Tighem, Kevin, 1952-
Wild animals of the Canadian Rockies / Kevin Van
Tighem ; [photographs by] Dennis & Esther Schmidt.

ISBN 978-1-897522-26-4

1. Mammals—Rocky Mountains, Canadian (B.C. and Alta.).
2. Mammals—Rocky Mountains, Canadian (B.C. and Alta.)—Pictorial
works. I. Schmidt, Dennis, 1921- II. Schmidt, Esther, 1922- III. Title.

QL221.R6V36 2009   599.09711
C2008-907158-1

Library of Congress Control Number: 2009920193

Cover: Grizzly bear
Back cover: Wolf cubs
Frontispiece: Gray wolf
P. 6: Cougar

Printed in Canada

Rocky Mountain Books acknowledges the financial support for its
publishing program from the Government of Canada through the
Book Publishing Industry Development Program (BPIDP), Canada
Council for the Arts, and the province of British Columbia through the
British Columbia Arts Council and the Book Publishing Tax Credit.

CONTENTS

- 8 -
Bears

- 18 -
Ungulates

- 36 -
Wild Cats

- 40 -
Wild Dogs

- 44 -
Small Mammals

- 51 -
Smallest Mammals

WILD ANIMALS

There was a time when no animals ranged the Canadian Rockies. It was not long ago, really — barely the blink of an eye as the Rockies, which have formed the spine of this continent for more than 45 million years, see time.

Immense glaciers filled every valley from northern B.C. south to what is now the Waterton-Glacier International Peace Park. Until only twelve thousand years ago, the mountains were islands of stone in a sea of ice. Glaciers filled the bottom of B.C.'s Rocky Mountain Trench and extended well into the Alberta foothills.

Strange animals lived within sight of those mountain glaciers. Herds of massive bison with long, spreading horns foraged on shrubby grasslands chilled by glacial winds. There they fended off attacks by dire wolves, animals twice as large as today's timber wolves. The herds of bison, giant sheep and small horses also fed huge coyotes, lions, scimitar cats, and a kind of long-legged bear that hunted in packs. Sabre-toothed cats stalked giant ground sloths. Bands of humans hunted mastodons. The sky, no doubt, was filled with the gabble of wild fowl.

Anyone who knows the Rockies and their wildlife today would have found it an alien landscape indeed—a miracle of wildlife diversity and abundance.

No scientist has yet managed to explain why so many animals became extinct about the time the mountain glaciers began to melt back. Why did dire wolves vanish while the smaller timber wolves survived? Why did the mastodon and giant bison disappear while vast herds of plains and wood bison lived on? The changing climate may have played a role. Spreading populations of human hunters almost certainly did.

Whatever the case, no one alive today can ever see the giant animals of the late Ice Age. They are gone.

Today's visitors to the Canadian Rockies must be content with the smaller modern bison, moose, elk and deer. Our predators are grizzly and black bears, wolves, coyotes, lynx and cougars—not the massive Ice Age predators. The most commonly seen wild animals in the Canadian Rockies—the small mammals—rarely inspire awe.

It was only ten or twelve thousand years ago that the glaciers melted back into the highest, coldest places. As the ice retreated, vegetation flooded up the valleys and cloaked the mountain slopes, and in the long, slow wash of time the modern landscapes of the Rockies emerged. A wealth of wildlife emerged, too: unique and specialized animals whose lives are intimately tied to the patterns and rhythms of today's high country.

The Canadian Rockies are a young landscape, populated by young wildlife species. But those wild animals are every bit as dramatic and remarkable in their own right as the now-extinct and seemingly more exotic creatures whose day has passed. The time will come when modern mammals—humans included—will follow the mastodon and the sabre-tooth into oblivion, giving way to even newer forms.

For now, however, the Canadian Rockies are home to at least 75 kinds of wild mammals. More than twenty protected areas—from Wild Kakwa, Willmore Wilderness and Jasper National Park south to Waterton Lakes National Park and B.C.'s Akamina-Kishinena Provincial Park—preserve the wilderness habitats of these species.

Two World Heritage Sites celebrate the ecological wealth of Canada's Rocky Mountains.

This is truly a special place. These are truly remarkable animals. Each species is a pinnacle of evolutionary history: a survivor where so many other species have failed and vanished. No one need regret the fact that we will never see the scimitar cats, giant bison and other strange megafauna that vanished a few thousand years ago.

The wild animals of today's Canadian Rockies are more than miracle enough.

BEARS

Humans and bears have shared the mountains for millennia. We have much in common, from our flat-footed tracks to our omnivorous diets and low reproductive rates.

First Nations people have long considered the bear an older brother. Bears taught aboriginal people which plants are good to eat or to use as medicines. In the legends of many tribes, the bear is a sacred animal that brought food to the people and showed them how to live.

Few people now experience the intimacy with animals that North America's aboriginal people once enjoyed. Like the early native people of the Rockies, modern Canadians fear wild bears. We no longer, however, respect them as older brothers.

In the brave light of day we watch bears from safety, as strangers seeking entertainment, thrilled by our fears. Both bear and human suffer from such estrangement. Humans lose because our fear and the shallowness of our understanding isolates us further from the wild, living world that is our true home. Bears lose because our fear and disrespect make them dangerous, and we kill them.

The Rocky Mountains remain a place of hope. Here, perhaps, we can re-learn the humility and respect that will make us, again, brother and sister to the bear.

Top: Bears range widely, foraging on roots, insects, newborn ungulates, grasses, berries, nuts and other foods.

Opposite: From April through early November, a black bear's sensitive nose leads it from one food source to another.

BLACK BEARS

More people see black bears than grizzlies, because black bears prefer the forested habitats where we have our roads, resorts and campgrounds. Black bears eat dandelions, horsetails and other plants that thrive on roadsides and other man-made habitats.

For thousands of years, black bears found rich pickings around the edges of human camps and settlements. Aboriginal people traditionally placed their dead on platforms in trees to protect them from scavenging bears. Their dogs cleaned up camp scraps. Native people had no choice but to prevent black bears from raiding their camps for food: the price of failure might be starvation or a fatal attack by a hungry bear grown bold.

Twentieth-century visitors to black bear country face a similar challenge. Today, however, most humans travel in motor vehicles, sleep behind walls, and need rarely cope with the consequences of our own failures. Today, concern for the well-being of black bears is what motivates us to keep them from becoming addicted to human food or garbage.

Park wardens kill fewer black bears than they used to. Modern garbage-handling systems protect bears from their fatal attraction to human food. Few tourists feed bears anymore—a sign of growing respect and understanding that bodes well for the black bear's future.

Top: Humped back, broad forehead and grizzled fur distinguish this grizzly from its relative, the black bear.

Opposite: A female grizzly and her two-year-old cubs test the air, uneasy about the human photographer nearby.

GRIZZLY BEARS

"Of grisly bears there are but too many," wrote explorer David Thompson two centuries ago. The grizzly bear gets its name from its grizzled fur, not a grisly nature. Many modern visitors to grizzly country, however, agree with Thompson. Fear of a bear attack keeps them from venturing into the wild.

In truth, however, there are probably too few grizzlies. Biologists warn that the great bear may soon vanish from some parts of the Canadian Rockies.

Grizzlies reproduce more slowly than almost any other animal. A female must survive at least five winters before breeding for the first time. She will have, on average, only two cubs every three years.

The grizzly's taste for open country may account for a mother grizzly's ferocity in defense of her cubs. Unlike the black bear, she cannot send her cubs up a tree when danger threatens.

Instead, the mother grizzly tries to frighten enemies away. If that fails, she attacks.

Once every year or so an unfortunate hiker surprises a female grizzly, triggering her protective instincts. The hiker may suffer injuries or death. The grizzly is usually hunted down and killed. Biologists warn that too many female grizzlies have died in recent years, as humans flood the high country. For now, Canada's Rockies remain a tenuous refuge for this wilderness species.

Top: Avalanche slopes, stream floodplains and other natural forest openings are among the open habitats grizzly bears prefer.

Right: Ears forward, this grizzly is watchful, but not upset.

Opposite: Grizzlies are intelligent, solitary animals that seek to avoid conflict with people.

Overleaf: There is no more dangerous wild animal in the Rockies than a female grizzly determined to protect her young cubs.

UNGULATES

What strange extravagance of Nature decreed that hoofed animals should carry great weights around on their heads? A bighorn ram's horns or a bull moose's antlers may weigh more than twenty kilograms. Ungulates must survive bitterly cold winters and deep snow. Heavy horns or antlers waste precious energy.

Only the males of most species can spare the energy needed to grow large antlers and horns. Females put all their energy into the precious fetuses growing in their bodies. Unlike males, they must accumulate body fat to nurture offspring.

The massive horns of a bighorn ram or the spreading antlers of a bull elk or mule deer buck are proof of superiority. Only animals with sufficient skill and strength to survive several years acquire such status symbols. Large horns or antlers prove that these males are healthy, of superior genetic stock, and likely to pass on their vigour to their offspring.

Ungulates mate in the fall. The males with the most impressive headgear do most of the breeding. Then, as winter snows accumulate and food becomes hard to find, the females and young gather on the best winter ranges. Exhausted males, their work done, retire to less friendly terrain. If they die of their own too-much or fall victim to predators, it matters little to the population. Next spring, a new generation will carry on their legacy.

Top: White-tailed deer frequent the aspen parkland and river-bottom forests of the larger valleys.

Opposite: Thousands of years of natural selection by wolves, cougars and humans have made the white-tailed deer exceptionally alert and fleet of foot.

Top: A rutting mule deer buck has a swollen neck and a steady, purposeful walk as he searches the November woods for does.

Right: A doe mule deer and her fawn listen in all directions for potential danger.

Opposite: A truly western deer, the mule deer is larger than the whitetail and frequents more open country.

Top: Elk, like other deer, grow new antlers each year. Large-antlered bulls —the most genetically superior, well-fed and prime-aged males—dominate smaller bulls.

Right: Cow elk and newborn calves gather into herds. More eyes and ears offer greater safety from predators.

Opposite: Each September, rutting bull elk fill the frosty mornings with frenzied bugling as they gather harems of cows and compete for breeding rights.

Top: A moose immerses its whole head to eat submerged pondweeds. This bull's growing antlers are covered with velvet.

Right: Cow moose: listening, smelling and watching for danger.

Opposite: A young bull moose displays its ponderous nose, palmate antlers, long legs and the characteristic—but seemingly useless—"bell" on its neck.

Top: Deep grooves mark each year's growth of a bighorn ram's horn. This full-curl ram is at least eight years old.

Left: Bighorns rarely feed on flat open ground. Their short legs make them vulnerable to surprise attacks by wolves or other predators.

Opposite: A mature ram's swollen neck and enlarged scrotum are signs of the November breeding season.

Top: Small-horned, younger rams give way to dominant, large-horned rams. They rarely enjoy much success in breeding.

Left: Within a few hours of birth, bighorn lambs can run, climb and clamber around on cliffs where they are safe from predators.

Top: In late fall, bighorn rams like this massive old-timer will cross broad valleys to travel from one concentration of ewes to another.

Left: Dominance battles result when rams of similar size compete for status. To gain power, both rams rise high on their hind legs.

Right: Upon contact, bodies telescope and necks curl under. Spongy bones at the base of the horns protect their brains.

Wild Animals of the Canadian Rockies · 29

Top: Spongy hoof pads, a low centre of gravity and an incredible ability to balance and turn enable mountain goats to perform astonishing climbing feats.

Right: Two layers of dense white wool protect mountain goats from wind and cold.

Opposite: Slow, methodical, incredibly tough: mountain goats thrive on the toughest terrain the Rockies have to offer.

Top: Late each spring, herds of nannies and their newborn kids travel to mineral licks to eat soil and replenish trace minerals. Athabasca River, Jasper National Park.

Opposite: A solitary mountain goat, safe from predators, seems unaware of the law of gravity.

Top: Herds of plains bison once wintered in the windblown grasslands along the flanks of the Rocky Mountains. Their grazing helped shape the native prairie.

Left: A lone bull bison. Only a few captive herds remain of the more than 60 million bison that once ranged the West.

Top: Mountain caribou bull: a species threatened by logging, roadkill and climate change. Small herds of caribou survive in Jasper National Park and farther north.

Right: Unlike other North American deer species, female caribou grow small antlers.

CATS

ats hunt alone by night, prowling the shadows and watching for prey. A cat's eyes are specialized for night work, equipped with cells that double the amount of light they see. Focussing on the slightest movement, a hunting cat freezes, crouches low, and fixes its prey with an uncanny stare.

Only three kinds of wild cat prowl the Canadian Rockies. The bobcat is least common, since this small cat has difficulty coping with winter snows. For lynx, on the other hand, deep snow is no problem. Their large, snowshoe-like feet enable them to hunt their favourite prey: the snowshoe hare. Even so, lynx are uncommon in the Rockies. The western mountains contain too few concentrations of snowshoe hares.

The cougar is the most abundant wild cat in the Rockies. Cougars stalk deer the way house cats stalk mice. One paw at a time, body low, eyes and ears fixed on its prey, the tawny shadow eases to within a few metres, then races from hiding. If luck is on its side, the cougar will grasp its prey around the shoulders with sharp-clawed forefeet and bite through its victim's neck. Most often, however, the cougar's quarry escapes unharmed.

Cougars are the most efficient deer predators in the Rockies, far outperforming the wolf. Wolves and bears, in fact, frequently steal cougar kills rather than going to the trouble of hunting their own prey.

Top: A female cougar and her kitten.

Opposite: Canada's largest wild cat, the cougar is widespread and common from Banff National Park south through shallow-snow regions of Alberta and B.C.

Top: Long legs and oversized feet enable the Canada lynx to hunt its favourite prey—the snowshoe hare—in deep winter snows.

Left: Bobcats are among the most rare of Rocky Mountain predators. Unlike lynx, they cannot cope with deep snow.

Opposite: Sensitive whiskers on their faces and the bottoms of their feet help wild cats feel their way through darkened forests.

DOGS

Late evening: the mountains are silhouetted against the fading sky. Shadows pool beneath the pines.

A coyote yelps. Another replies; then a hysterical cacophony of barks and shrieks shatters the evening calm.

Far off—beginning on a low note, rising gradually, then trailing away forlornly—a more fearsome voice issues from the shadows. The silence after the wolf howl is brittle with expectancy. Every animal in the valley, no doubt, has paused for a moment to test the breeze and listen. The coyotes remain discreetly silent. Something will die tonight.

Of all predators, the wild dogs arouse the strongest human emotions. Sociable, intelligent predators, wolves and coyotes have survived a century of persecution. Eradicated in the 1950s, wolves recently recolonized the southern Rockies. The smaller red fox is no doubt as glad of the wolf's return as are raven, magpie, chickadee and wolverine. All scavenge meals from the remains of winter wolf kills.

Wolf packs kill animals as big as moose. Such large prey requires teamwork to kill, providing more than enough meat for pack members to share. Foxes hunt alone. Their small prey requires no teamwork and provides no leftovers.

The adaptable coyote can adopt either lifestyle. When small mammals are abundant, coyotes hunt alone. When winter snows make deer vulnerable, coyotes form small packs and hunt big game.

Top: Sharp-nosed, big-eared and intelligent, the coyote usually hunts mice and small animals. Packs of coyotes, however, can kill deer or even small elk.

Opposite: A timber wolf howls to communicate with other pack members. Less common than the coyote, wolves have recently recolonized most of the Canadian Rockies, as far south as Montana.

Top: Wolves are built for travel. Packs range widely across the landscape, hunting deer, elk and other large prey.

Left: A young wolf focusses ears, eyes and nose on a possible meal.

Top: Fox kits, like other young dogs, chew at the lips of returning parents. The chewing triggers a gag reflex, and the adult regurgitates a partly digested meal for the hungry kit.

Right: The fox relies on acute hearing and a finely tuned nose to find mice and other small prey.

SMALL MAMMALS

Fur trappers penetrated the Canadian Rockies in the early 1800s. They soon came to hate the wolverine. Wolverines, however, welcomed this new kind of human. Wolverines must travel widely and scavenge aggressively, especially in winter, to find enough food. Trappers made life easier by setting steel traps along the mountain valleys for marten, fisher, mink and other creatures. Wolverines quickly learned to rob traplines and raid trappers' cabins.

Trapping's time is mostly past in the Rockies. Martens and fishers now face more danger from logging than cold steel. Wolverines have had to revert to old ways of finding food. Some of the highest concentrations of wolverines persist along the Continental Divide: in the Yoho Valley, Lake Louise area and Akamina-Kishinena region of B.C. It is no coincidence that another mid-sized animal—the porcupine—is common there. In midwinter, a hungry wolverine will gladly chance a face full of quills for a meal of fat-rich porcupine meat.

Porcupines remain active all winter because their preferred food—the sapwood of trees—is always available. Beavers, which also eat tree bark, build underwater caches of twigs and freshly cut branches so they can continue to eat after the ponds freeze. Hoary marmots, whose high timberline and alpine meadows produce a wealth of greenery in summer, simply curl up in their dens and sleep the hungry winter away.

Top: A beaver recycles an aspen tree into food and construction materials.

Opposite: Beavers cut down aspens to build dams and to eat the bark and twigs. After a year or two, their aspen supply exhausted, the large rodents die or move on. The aspen re-sprout from their roots; eventually beavers return.

Top: Raccoons have only invaded the Rockies recently. They remain rare, confined to river-bottoms at low elevations.

Left: Foraging near water, raccoons leave distinctive hand-like tracks in mud.

Top: Porcupines are common in some timberline areas in the Rockies. They feed on bark and twigs.

Right: Dense guard hairs conceal a forest of barbed quills which protect the porcupine when predators threaten.

Top: The wolverine, a threatened species, survives throughout the Canadian Rockies. This determined hunter and scavenger is the largest member of the weasel family.

Left: Badgers are built for digging. Long claws and powerful leg muscles enable them to dig up and kill ground squirrels and gophers.

Top: Threatened by logging in many areas, the American marten thrives in the old-growth forests of Canada's mountain national parks and other protected areas.

Right: Fishers are rare in the Rockies. They prefer low elevation old-growth forest where they hunt hares, squirrels and porcupines.

SMALLEST MAMMALS

A deer mouse may give birth three or more times a year. A single pair of deer mice could theoretically multiply to more than 600 within twelve months.

Small mammals like deer mice live short lives and breed prolifically. They are abundant, too; many more small mammals can occupy the same space as only a few larger mammals. A grizzly bear, for example, may have a home range of more than a thousand km². Within that bear's home range, there are millions of mice, squirrels, chipmunks and ground squirrels.

It is fortunate, and no coincidence, that small mammals are so abundant. Grizzly bears need not worry about being eaten. Smaller mammals, on the other hand, provide meals for hawks, eagles, prairie falcons, owls, martens, badgers, weasels, coyotes, foxes, lynx and many other animals.

Mountain winters are hard. Small mammals must fatten and reproduce during the short period between April and October when vegetation is most lush. Some, like pikas and woodrats, store dried vegetation during the summer so they can eat during the long winter. Others, like chipmunks and ground squirrels, hibernate in underground dens all winter. Mice and voles hide beneath the insulating snow cover. Only the red squirrel remains active above the snow to greet winter visitors to the Rockies.

Top: Snowshoe hares thrive in willow tangles and recently burned forests.

Opposite: Bouldery meadows near timberline are home to the hoary marmot, whose piercing alarm whistle alerts passing hikers to the nearby presence of the large rodents.

Top: Three species of chipmunk thrive in the forests and shrub thickets of the Canadian Rockies.

Left: Deer mice are the most abundant of several species of mice and voles that serve as prey for coyotes, martens, weasels, hawks, owls and other predators.

Top: Commonly misidentified as a chipmunk, the golden-mantled ground squirrel has a distinctive eye ring and buff-coloured shoulders.

Right: Pikas are tiny rabbits that scurry about gathering and drying grass all summer long. Pikas store their hay in boulder piles. Beneath the snow-pack, they feed on it all winter long.

Top: Richardson's ground squirrel thrives in shortgrass prairie along the flanks of the Rockies.

Left: The red squirrel is the only tree-dwelling squirrel in the Rockies. Common and noisy, it is fiercely territorial.

Top: Columbian ground squirrels stand erect and squeak when they spot potential danger on the ground. Passing hawks and eagles evoke a different response: the rodents dive for the safety of their burrows.

Bottom right: In the Rockies, thirteen-lined ground squirrels live only in the bunchgrass prairie of Waterton Lakes National Park.

Bottom left: All ground squirrels hibernate. This one is gathering nesting material for its underground winter den.

THE AUTHOR

Through his writings, Kevin Van Tighem communicates his passion for the creatures that inhabit the alpine wilderness. Having worked in Banff, Jasper, Yoho, Elk Island, Waterton Lakes, Glacier and Mt. Revelstoke national parks for the Canadian Parks Service and the Canadian Wildlife Service, he has come to know and love the wildlife of the Canadian

Rockies. In his numerous magazine articles and his book, *Wild Animals of Western Canada*, he describes the beauty and integrity of the animals with a sense of awe and wonder.

PHOTOGRAPHERS

Dennis and Esther Schmidt's commitment to wildlife photography has been a life-long endeavour. Together, they have travelled across Western Canada, forging

intimate relationships with the landscape and the wildlife it supports. That they have been full-time photographers for twenty years testifies to their love for working outdoors in the Rocky Mountains; the beauty of their images is evidence of their talent.